MONEY

BLUES

TO

BLUE

MONEY

Josgh —
Happy manifesting

King

More Books by Ming Chee:

Being Present to Serve
(co-authored with Amina Makhdoom)

Reiki Fur Babies
(co-authored with Candy Boroditsky)

Ming Chee

MONEY BLUES TO BLUE MONEY

ALCHEMY FOR CREATING EVERLASTING WEALTH

"Therefore, it is important to remain open to all possibilities, for you never know how the Universe can deliver something to you. It may only be after the fact that you realize you have been given a truly precious gift from your higher self." – Richard Dotts

This is for everyone
who has, or is,
struggling with
money. To know that
if I can make it,
anyone can.

A special heartfelt *Thank You* to my
editor, Lori Aldana.

FOREWORD

I started reading this book and knew from the first page I wouldn't be able to put it down. It's a fun and easy read (never thought that the word "fun" and "finance" would ever be put in the same sentence). The information Dr. Ming Chee shares is like nothing I've ever read before—and I've read many on building financial wealth. It gives a totally different perspective to why some people never seem to get around the lack of money and others are abundantly wealthy. Also, for those who are wealthy and still not satisfied with money. Her information is the MISSING LINK to those who've tried forever to get on track and move into abundance, but just never seem to get there. I hadn't even finished this book and was thinking, *"How soon will the next book come out?"* I provide life coaching and will be using this book for all my clients who are struggling financially.

It's a life changer...highly recommended!!

Sally Thalia, Intuitive

CONTENTS

FOREWORD i

INTRODUCTION v

CH 1 ~ BEING SEEN 1

CH 2 ~ MONEY SAYS 14

CH 3 ~ MASTERING MONEY MENTALITY 24

CH 4 ~ THE MONEY ALLERGY 46

CH 5 ~ MANIFESTING MONEY 58

CH 6 ~ FINANCIAL MAGIC 70

CH 7 ~ LOVE AND MONEY 84

CH 8 ~ GIVING AND RECEIVING 100

CH 9 ~ LAST BUT NOT LEAST, HOW DO YOU KEEP THE MONEY FLOWING IN? 113

CONCLUSION 119

INTRODUCTION

It takes just 17 seconds of FOCUS to activate a thought.

Abraham Hicks says a thought reaches a combustion point at 17 seconds of pure undiluted focus. That thought then draws another thought to it and it is exponentially more powerful.

At the end of another 17 seconds, 34 seconds total, the next thought combusts, and by the Law of Attraction, evolves to a higher level of energy.

To activate your mind into alignment with Money, I'd like you to begin with a test run using this Money mantra. I chose this mantra because you picked up this book to help get over your Money blues.

A 17-second read-through should be good to activate the right vibe and get you on your way to making a shift as you start reading this book. After seventeen seconds, honor any inspiration afterwards to keep on track.

Money comes to me easily. Money comes to me so easily it literally comes out of the BLUE!
Money comes in all shapes, sizes, colors, and smells.
Money surrounds me wherever I go.
Money loves to be with me. Money loves to delight me.
Money loves to hear me squeal with joy as it appears.
Money comes in free lunches. Money comes in from my friends and family. Money even comes from strangers.
Money comes from angels so effortlessly. Did you see that coin left for you on the street?
Money smells so good. Not just the crisp smell of a new dollar bill. You can smell Money in food, or in a really nice glass of wine, or in a bite of rich decadent chocolate.
Money comes in the form of a new

bank loan, a car deal, a new mortgage rate. Money is endless!

Money says, "I am here—lets have some fun together."

Money says, "I am magical. Let me show you the ways I love you."

Above all, Money is FREE. Let it be. Believe it to be so, and Money is YOURS.

CH 1 ~ BEING SEEN

My personal journey with Money has been one of many layers unfolding. My story is well known throughout my close friends, family, and the people who participated in the online Money coaching and support group called Being Present to Serve (BPS)—which became sort of a pilot for The Money Alchemist to emerge. Now, I want to share my story with you because I went through a major shift, an overhaul. And made a complete 360. Not 180. I came full circle from what I thought I knew about Money to personally getting to know Money.

I'll begin with a flawed belief I was very attached to growing up and it had to do with — you guessed it.

Money.

Money in my family was a means for showing love. Yet, sometimes it was also a form of control. It took several shapes and roles in my family, and I was never quite sure about Money when it came around me. Especially from family. There were many times when I found myself unable to accept Money being given or offered to me within the family without feeling 'icky' about it.

Fast forward many years later. In 2012, during Christmas, it rained on me. No, not Money. I mean like one life-altering storm after another testing my strength and courage for survival. Life took a turn for me when my husband got laid off earlier that year. A position in San Francisco opened up for him. Great! Except we were living in Los Angeles. But, we saw other couples doing the whole long-distance relationship thing, so we figured we could, too.

Initially, I would fly over on weekends to see him and when I couldn't, we called and emailed each other. Without noticing too much, the intervals in between us seeing each other and communicating became longer. Until one day he stopped communicating. The communication depended on me.

Then the holidays came. Thanksgiving turned out horrible. And I'll just say it had nothing to do with the food. Christmas, though, was a holiday we loved to share because he introduced me to special traditions. So, I went out of my way to get a beautiful tree, nice gifts, and delicious spread of food. On Christmas morning he was gone. No good-bye. No note. Nothing.

Well, it goes without saying, I had a $4,000 mortgage and all the bills that come with a house—gardener, insurance, car payment, a ton of bills. It got to the point where I was eating out of a box. Meaning, I was buying Lean Cuisine meals for a $1 each. I had 3 priorities:

- Somehow, I keep my house for my Labrador Sammy Diva's sake because of health reasons;
- I feed my two fur babies without compromising their special diet;
- I maintain a *Money Coach*. I stress Money Coach here because without Jeannette, the Good Vibe Coach, I don't know where I'd be today.

Back to my limited beliefs surrounding Money. Because I believed Money was attached to control and status in our family, I taught myself not to talk about it with my parents. As such, I also didn't share my life with my parents in case they would not fully support me when it came to me and Money. And that meant even during these turbulent times of financial struggle.

Throughout years of conditioning my relationship with my parents I had learned to be for them what they wanted to see me as. I am their daughter, a "successful pharmacist with a doctorate degree." If I went to them for help, financial help, I would only disappoint them, especially my father, and I would feel out of alignment accepting Money from him.

Instead, I leaned on my metaphysical beliefs and spiritual family to weather the storms. I only wanted to be surrounded by those who supported my divine purpose. I didn't feel like my purpose was to be head of a prominent hospital's pharmacy department. If anyone asked me what it is I am, I would have rather said a healer, a Reiki Master, a Money Alchemist, a coach, someone who inspires others to follow their divine purpose and gives back to the world.

Naturally, I never thought my father would ever see that in me. In fact, I pretty much had given up on it. I didn't feel bad about it either. I just let go. I found a spiritual family who "saw" ME. I managed to build an emotional balance between my spiritual family and my natural family, mainly my parents, that I felt I was happy with.

Then the unfathomable occurred.

Something transformed during one weekend when I was at a family reunion. My parents were getting close to turning 80 years old. It was an important gathering. It wasn't easy either to get all of us together now as adults and my brothers with wives and children...but we all managed to make the time.

One night at dinner my Dad asked me about my role in Reiki Fur Babies which is an energy healing practice that my best friend/business partner, Candy, and I founded. He asked me when it had been that I was on TV promoting RFB. I laughed because I didn't even realize he remembered I was on TV on a Colorado station. I told him it was years ago. I didn't really elaborate. And he asked no further.

The next morning, I was reading the posts from the BPS group and I was so touched and moved by what people were sharing about who they ARE and what service they were bringing to the world. Suddenly, I had this amazing clarity to share with my Dad what it was I was doing. It was so profoundly clear. I looked from the bedroom I was in and could see my Dad sitting alone in the living room. I took my laptop because something in me said to show him besides just telling him. I asked him if he had a few minutes to listen to what I was doing.

As I shared with him about how I met Amina, my BPS spiritual partner and sister, he was like WOW. I shared with him the vision we both had and how the group was born. How we make Money. How we teach others to make Money. How we wrote a book. I showed him our Facebook page. My Dad was clearly impressed.

He asked, "You have these many people in your group?"

He continued, "All these people, they all want to serve the planet and give back?"

I replied with excitement, "Yes!"

He then said he wanted to read our book. Seriously, by this time I was already in shock and almost in tears because he *saw* ME. He really got it. Not only did he get it, he wanted to support it.

On that day, such a profound healing took place between my Dad and me, in what began with a moment of clarity and following my heart.

The next thing he asked me was, "How may I show you what I'm working on to give back?" After thinking about it for a second, he then shared with me who his business partners were and the important work they were doing.

It was a full circle of healing. A miracle I never expected. It sure feels good to be *seen* completely.

Which brings me to ask you:

Are YOU being seen?

Are you stepping into your divine gifts?

It is important to be honest with ourselves because when we allow ourselves to do that, we are seeing ourselves. When we see ourselves, we allow the Universe to see us.

This is the first lesson on how the Money comes in; the abundance; all we need.

It is vital that WE see ourselves.

Once we allow ourselves to be seen by ourselves, others see what we see. So, look at yourself with love in your heart and see what you have to offer to the Universe.

When I was living in Los Angeles, I was not being fully seen. There were many times I felt invisible. I didn't even realize it until I moved to another state because I didn't have the awareness of what it meant to really be seen. I did know this much, I was not being seen and I didn't know why.

Moving to a new city, where nobody knew me or what I did, I allowed myself to step into what I connected with, what made me feel alive—a Reiki Master, teacher and healer for animals.

Candy and I joined the Chamber of Commerce where we could talk and share with others about what we did and who we are.

It was natural to reply, "We are Reiki Masters who work with animals."

It was so easy and effortless.

There was no fear.

There was no thinking what will people think? Will they know what Reiki is?

None of those thoughts came up. In fact, the opposite. In fact, at the first meeting at the Chamber, people came up to us and said, "Wow! Reiki Masters. That is so cool." Now, everywhere we go, people ask us what we do, and we reply authentically just who we are what we do.

It is universal law that when we step into our divine gifts the Universe must back us up. Why must it? Because the Universe is always *responding* to us.

By doing what we love, stepping into our divine gifts, we meet the right people, we get the emails, situations and opportunities appear that are perfect for what we need. Inspiration hits, intuition comes in. All we need to do is step into who we are, our authentic self, and the Universe backs us up.

The journey to becoming the Money Alchemist was effectively the same journey as Reiki Fur Babies. I just kept doing what I was doing. A lot of the requests I got from people surrounded Money. Once I participated in a call with my Money coach on how to manifest $1000 in 10 days, from then on, I kept on doing coaching calls all about manifesting Money. I started by noticing in myself how I was able to create abundance in my life.

Once I realized HOW I was manifesting abundance, it never stopped.

It kept coming.

The Universe delivered again and again.

Another example, I met my BPS partner Amina on a lark really. Though divinely orchestrated. That day, we spoke on the phone for 90 minutes talking about ourselves and our beliefs and how much we loved to serve others.

Out of that phone call we created a 6-week free program called Being Present to Serve—How We Make Money. Then we created a support group and it became even clearer.

Up until then, I had not really wrap my head around any of the specifics I was doing in my "coaching." In fact, I asked our group what they felt the sessions revolved around, and that is when alchemy came up.

So, I encourage you—if you want to manifest more Money into your life, continue to step into those divine gifts and allow the Universe to back you up. Allow yourself to be SEEN.

Remember where I was in 2012, when I was in all that contrast. I had a $4000 mortgage, property taxes, bills all around me—the list was endless. I had so many things I was trying to juggle, let alone put food on the table for myself. Thinking back, it wasn't even much long ago.

What is important to note is there were several things I put into practice and have still been practicing over the years. Practicing and practicing principles and affirmations, until they became part of me. I'm excited to share them with you here.

Easy does it. My motto for just about everything. NO attachment. When you let go of control and strings of attachment to a situation, it lets in the bigger and better things. Better job, better living situation, even better friends. Keep it light, easy and loose. **Feel better first. ALWAYS.** Raising your vibe is about what we feel is important.

If I am feeling slightly off, I look for a faster way of getting back to my core values of peace and joy.

Inner guidance always rules! When I learned to trust my guides and the Universe, my inner guidance became my compass for every situation.

Weed out tolerations. Anything negative going on around me—you just might see me walking out the door. I do not need to tolerate negativity.

Question negative thoughts. Sure, we are human, they come in. But we can release them as well. We don't have to stay there. We can choose.

Go Pollyanna. (Hey, Pollyanna is a badass.) Appreciation of all the wonderful things in our lives, even when we are in contrast, is not an easy feat. But optimism always brings in the magic.

Make friends with contrast. Whenever I feel doubtful or not being able to see something in a positive light, I change the view to a more positive perspective. I add the hashtag #loveithere to my social media posts and it turns everything around. I use this hashtag for everything.

Keep your energetic environment clean. This is a big one. Ever since I became very aware of what and who was around me, it changed my life. It even brought in new guides, new friends, new everything.

This is how Money came in for me, and still comes in. I continue to remain open to the delights headed my way.

CH 2 ~ MONEY SAYS

Forming bonds and close relationships is natural behavior in human beings, an instinct even. When we begin a new relationship with someone the first thing we do is get to know that person. We ask them questions to get a feel for them and see if we're on the same wave length. Could we be friends?

Sometimes we want to know someone only as far as the front door, so we don't ask too many questions.

Other times, we feel a connection and we want to befriend that person, finding things we have in common and build on that.

Then there are people with whom we become more intimate with. We explore, we share, we give of ourselves to them.

I got thinking about the relationships we as human beings forge with Money. So, I asked myself, *what would Money say to me?*

Tuning into the energy of Money, I was reminded of a blog written by my Money coach entitled *Is your Money Having Fun*. It inspired me to look at Money as energy with much more facets than simply a piece of paper with a dollar value.

Feeling and connecting to Money's vibration it told me Money wants to be happy. Not only does it want to be happy, it wants EVERYONE to be happy when spending it, giving it, investing it, thinking about it, borrowing it, loaning it, receiving it.

Think about it. How many times have you been reluctant, hesitant, or afraid when it comes to Money? Is it too much Money, not enough, should I borrow? Should I spend, could I spend? Should I? Would I? Those vibrations drain Money away.

Flat out Money wants to be happy. Money is a happy energy. Think of it like this—when you are happy you are vibrating happiness. Because Money is a happy energy it is attracted to that same vibration. It's a like attracts like thing.

Wouldn't it be cool if you could talk to Money...and make it your friend?

Yes.

And, yes, you certainly can.

One day, I asked the question on a group call, "If you could interview Money what would you ask?" I took the inspiration from a movie starring Will Smith called *Collateral Beauty* in which he talks to Death, Time, and Love. By asking the group this question, even just thinking about the question, opened such an awareness in them they didn't even realize existed.

Their interview questions to Money were both practical and intimate. The responses we received from Money were truly kind, loving, and supportive. I'm going to share the questions and answers with you here.

When you read these, I encourage you to open your mind and your heart as though you are being introduced to Money for the first time. This is your opportunity to become acquainted with Money and connect one on one on an entire different level. Hopefully, you will be inviting Money to cross the threshold past your front door.

Interview with Money

If you could pick one emotion which best describes you, what would it be?

Money says: Extraordinary.

What do people say to make you stay

away?

Money says: People get frustrated and angry at Money. People think Money is evil and bad.

What is your favorite characteristic of a billionaire?

Money says: The love of Money and feeling connected and pursued. Imagine what it feels like when you want to be with someone and you can't because they don't love you enough. Money wants to be with everyone. But not everyone wants to be with Money.

Money, many in the world want to know you, yet to them you seem very illusive. What is the most common thing people misunderstand about you?

Money says: That we are separated.

What is your favorite method of communicating with those who desire to connect with you?

Money says: To Love the Self.

Beloved Money when are you coming home? How can we use our combined gifts to change our family's destiny? How can we change the world?

Money says: By embracing our Self-

*worthiness which is related to letting
me come in. Don't stop Money at the
door. Feel worthy of Money.*
Money do you really exist, and why do
people associate you with power?
*Money says: Because they "get to"
experience a momentary sense of
freedom. They don't understand my
real meaning. They just focus on having
me in 3D, so they can feel free for a
moment's pleasure. Someone who
doesn't understand Money will buy a
new pair of shoes, feel good for a few
days, but then buyer's remorse sets in.
They don't understand you can't waste
Money. I do exist, and I am more than
just paper with value. I am an energy
with no more power than you have.*
Money if you took a holiday from earth
what would happen to the world?
*Money says: Money would change form
but there would be always something
to use for exchange, like bartering.
Money is paper, coins, a blanket. It is all
reciprocity.*
Why does Money exist? What is
Money's original purpose? Where is the

Money jar?

Money says: Money gives us the ability to trade for another source, like food, clothes, housing. It is for receiving and giving. As long as you remain connected to source, always giving and receiving...that is the basis for Money.

Who are you your parents? What is your first priority? How would you spend your last day on earth?

Money says: Who are your parents and where did you come from? [laughs] We all come from Source. Money would love to Flow to every being in all kinds of currency. Money's priority is bringing joy and abundance. You come with nothing you leave with nothing...so Money is here for you to play and to enjoy, and to bring happiness.

What turns you on? What kind of people do you love to hang with? Who's your best friend?

Money says: Money loves to hang out with people who appreciate and love me. Money is turned on when someone realizes the magic that is possible when we are partnered up.

How shall I honor you?

Money says: By honoring Yourself. By embracing and enjoying me.

Money, what is your favorite thing to do?

Money says: To be alive in peoples' heart.

What is your greatest fear?

Money says: No fear

How do you deal with abuse/corruption?

Money says: Man must heal their misperception. Money only has rewards.

What would you be when grown up?

Money says: Money is already grown up. It is a perfect reward from the Universe. Energy ascended.

Money what do you find is the most challenging about humans?

Money says: Humans want to hoard Money. Not letting it in and out, like breathing. Hoarding is adultery of abundance.

What is your primary love language?

Money says: All the love languages such as gift giving, quality time, words of affirmation, acts of service (devotion), and physical touch.

Money gave us a powerful revelation.

Money says it wants to be happy and it wants YOU to be happy...

When you are spending it.

When you are giving it.

When you are investing it.

When you are thinking about it.

When you are borrowing it.

When you are loaning it.

When you are receiving it.

Whatever it is that you are doing with Money, BE HAPPY with it.

Just think about all the things which make you happy. Whether it be puppies or any kind of animal, chocolate, a call from a good friend, flowers, walk on the beach, sex, movies, dancing, running, sports, singing, gardening, good food, wine, beer, ice cream! Getting the picture? Yes, all those things making you happy—is the same feeling Money wants to give to you.

Next time you have Money in your hands, have a chat with it. Embrace it. Get to know it better. You might even say, "Money, you know how much I love you—your energy, your gifts to my life, your color, your scent, and the feel of you in my hand."

Then watch how Money responds to you.

CH 3 ~ MASTERING MONEY

MENTALITY

I read the following excerpt in *A Course in Miracles Made Easy*:

> *"If you can realize how rich you already are, the car will show up as a manifestation of your wealth mentality. Like love, there are no external prerequisites to the experience of wealth. All the riches you could ever desire already exist right where you stand. Remember that you are deprived of nothing."*

This really got me thinking about the mentality of wealth. It is to do with mindset. Wealth is a mindset. Therefore, abundance is a mindset.

Psychologists tell us that the subconscious cannot distinguish between reality and imagination. The images we impress upon our mind, especially when accompanied by emotion, yield the same experience whether they are true or fictional. Applying this to manifesting money, it means when we tune into a wealth mindset, our brain picks it up as though it is our reality. Our brain then starts to pull in that abundance or wealth or whatever it is we want to manifest.

One day I decided I wanted to purchase a VW Jetta Wagon before I had seen one on the street. Suddenly, I am seeing them everywhere. I notice them in the parking lot, next to me on the road, even in TV commercials.

I love how our minds are THAT powerful.

What we focus on grows.

This is the mere fact why we should focus on love, on joy, on abundance, on service. Focusing on all of those feel good emotions and actions brings more of it to us. Some high vibrational words to bring us into a wealth mind set are words like gratitude, laughter, kindness, love, abundance, joy, freedom, compassion. These are just a few of the ones that come to mind instantly. It just takes focus to come up with your own. Sit with the thought and let the words come to you.

To master anything, all it takes is practice. I want you to fully jump in with practicing developing a strong wealth mindset.

Thoughts become things.

Align yourself to that acknowledgment. I say it all the time. But it is important to realize it as well. Notice it.

No matter what you are thinking those thoughts become energy.

Tangible.

If you think loving thoughts, they flow like radio waves in the sea of creation. If you think anxious thoughts, they flow the same way. So, if you are focused on lack, guess what? You will get more of that.

Ah. But what if you focus on love, on abundance, on fun? You will get more of that!

It works both ways.

When I decided that I wanted a new car, literally, the Universe conspired to give me it. It happened so fast there was no taking back the decision. It shocked me. I had never expected it to happen and manifest so quickly. I had all the reasons for wanting it. I had been rolling around the thought in my head for a little while but had not made the final decision. Until, I woke up one morning and thought *yes, I want a new car*. I made the decision then and there.

Out of the blue, I had people offering Money for my current car. *My goodness,* I thought, *I really need to pay close attention to my thoughts!* Then I set an intention for the perfect salesman to come to me. I had originally hoped to have my friend's car salesman, but he didn't react fast enough. The Universe brought someone to me.

No struggling, no striving. No stress. No hassles. No games.

The salesman sent me some emails and the best deals he could come up with. I decided on the car and next thing you know I'm on my way to picking up my new car.

Like I tell all my clients: Pay attention to your thoughts.

Your thoughts are very powerful especially when combined with eclipse energy, ah, and those fairies—manifesting is lightning fast for them. I'll talk more about elementals later because it's important to grasp the importance of awareness to our thoughts before I begin to talk to you about the magic.

Awareness is key to removing Money blocks.

When I work with my clients on kicking Money blocks to the curb the first thing I tell them is they are already half-way there. You are already thinking about making Money come to you, so you're on the right track. Except what you don't realize is that you have put a block up and stopped Money in its tracks by attaching limiting thoughts to Money.

When those gremlins or muggle thoughts pop into your head talking to you about scarcity and lack, you can tell them, "No, that is just a limiting belief and no longer a thought I choose to carry!"

These are a few of the most popular limiting thoughts, or Money Blocks, as I call them. If any of them sound familiar to you, you need to tell them to go away.

If I spend my Money, I won't have any left and end up in financial ruin.
I should be making a lot of Money by now.
I feel frustrated that Money isn't flowing in quickly and easily.
More Money is going out than coming in.
I feel anxious whenever I have to spend

Money.
Spending Money is being irresponsible.
I have to do things I don't enjoy in
order to make Money.
I have to work hard for Money.
Money takes sacrifice.
I have to work long hours for Money.
I have to be away from home to make
Money.
I am not worthy of Money.
Women cannot make lots of Money.

Those thoughts are low vibrating thoughts and do not reside with Money. If any of these thoughts are rolling around in your head, kick them to the curb and replace with high vibrating thoughts. You no longer choose to carry these thoughts around.

Speak your dreams out loud into being so they can become your reality.

YOU are the co-creator, the guardian of your happiness.

It's time to believe in amazing possibilities because they are in your future.

Inspire that hope. Hope always replenishes and uplifts.

It doesn't matter if your goals are simple or complex, as long as you spend every day living well. The life you live right now is the result of everything you have thought. If this life is not what you want, it is time you live it well. Not with limiting thoughts and beliefs and within "your means." Live well outside of all those confining thoughts and live in an expansive, creative, and loving Universe that is waiting for you to say the word.

There is a book by Rick Hanson, Ph.D. entitled *Buddha's Brain: The Practical Neuroscience of Happiness, Love, and Wisdom*. My favorite chapter is where he talks about having a "Mud Room" in your mind. A mud room is the place in your home you enter and remove your dirty shoes, take off your heavy coat, and leave all the baggage so as not to disrupt the rest of the home.

In a sense, the mud room in our mind is a place where our thoughts enter a space where we can unload them so as not to get knocked off our center.

I loved the thought of that.

Whatever passes through your mind is held in a spaciousness and in effect you aren't thrown off balance by negative or limited thoughts. Rather, we leave them in the mud room, so we can keep centered and stay in our sweet spot in alignment to what brings in the Money.

*"Equanimity is a perfect,
unshakable balance of mind."*
—Nyanaponika Thera

Dr. Hanson reflects on the above quote by stating:

*"Equanimity is neither apathy nor
indifference: you are warmly
engaged with the world but not
troubled by it. Through its
nonreactivity, it creates a great
space for compassion, loving-
kindness, and joy at the good
fortune of others."*

It is not that we don't care. This is not what he means or what the quote suggests. How I interpret it is that we can choose to transcend the experiences which do not serve us. Be aware of them but give them space without disenchantment, dissatisfaction, or disappointment. In this way we remain balanced and centered.

What a great place for some of our thoughts to hang out—in the mud room.

The wonderful thing about this is as you practice being mindful, your brain changes. As you tune into joy, your brain wires itself to joy.

When this happens, you start to see the world differently.

What you focus on grows.

Try out this mud room in the brain and see how you do. I think this is going to be a game changer.

Life is supposed to be fun. Life is for us to live to our highest potential. Joy and abundance are our natural state of being. It is our birthright and we can claim it. A good life is a creative and abundant life. As conscious creators we get to choose what we want.

We choose how we want to feel.

We choose what we want to see.

Money is energy. It is important to remember that.

When you are in fear, distrust, impatience and worry you are sending a signal to the Universe that you are not trusting. When fear, distrust, impatience, and worry are released you are allowing, giving permission, for all the good things to come to you.

The good things you are aligned with will come to you.

When you are in alignment, then your desires start happening spontaneously. When you are feeling good, when you are feeling joy, when you are in the flow—that is where the Money is.

That is the CERTAINTY of Money.

That is the energy of Money.

So, even when things look dire; trust. Trust that all is working out perfectly. You can do this. It takes practice—like everything else you learned and mastered.

Practice. Practice. Practice.

My BFF has a mantra, "Move through fear." If something scares her, she doesn't run away from it, instead she moves TOWARD it. The first time I realized she did that, it kind of freaked me out. Why would you move towards something that scares you?

We were in Banff heli-hiking one year and we got to the edge of a cliff. We had guides with us, but they did not tell us we were going to have to *swing* to the other side. *Seriously?!* I thought. There was no going back. I was terrified. I looked to my friend and I could see the concern on her face. Rather than turn around, she moved towards it. I do believe her husband wasn't exactly excited about it either. But we all did it. And I got the greatest picture of her flying across to the other side.

Later on, I decided to address my fear of drowning. Growing up in Washington, the water was always too cold for me. Occasionally, I swam in a lake, but mainly the only way my parents could get me to swim was by way of a heated pool or unheated smack in the middle of summer. I still remember the pool. I hated the feeling of being in the deep and the feeling of not being able to breathe under water. As it turns out, I have discovered I did drown in a past life! So, I made the decision to move towards the fear in this lifetime. I became a certified diver. Crazy as it sounds.

To qualify for the class, I had to swim 8 lengths of a pool without stopping. Now mind you, I am not a strong swimmer because I didn't like to swim when I was young. But after work I would drive to the YMCA and practice. When it came time to qualify, I passed. Next came the ocean part of it. A friend suggested I should get certified in warm water. Great idea. I headed to Belize where the water was like bath water.

The first test was to go 30 feet below—on my knees. The first time I did it, I freaked out and swam to the top of the ocean. In tears, I headed back to the boat. But I was still determined to push through and not give up. I was going to move toward my fear no matter what. I did it. I passed.

Why am I sharing this?

Fear should not limit you. You can move towards it and push through. This is how you can have what you desire. Believe everything is possible. That possibility begins within you.

You Choose.

You Allow.

You Believe It to Be True.

You Align.

You Become What You Intend.

You can do this. I have gone diving all over the world. Tahiti was my favorite. Ninety feet deep—yes, me. I went down that deep and saw the most amazing creatures. If I can move towards fear, you can, too.

Fear is a perception.

What is perception?

It is how we see and understand what occurs around us and what we decide those events will mean.

Our perception of reality can be a source of strength or weakness. The way it is decided is through the choice we make. We choose.

We have choices.

We can choose now how we want to feel.

We can choose and let life be easier.

Just like when I chose to change my perception about being in deep water and conquered my fear. Only then was I able to experience the beauty of the ocean.

If you want to experience the beauty of Money you are going to need to change your perception about it and how you obtain it, spend it, deal with it.

I love this analogy I came up with from Cinderella's fairytale. Cinderella did not ask to be rescued from her situation. She did not ask her stepmother and stepsisters to agree. She only asked for what she wanted—to go the ball. She didn't think about the how, about the logistics, or analyze the situation. What did she get? She got a FAIRY Godmother! That is how it works with manifesting what you want.

I came across an excerpt which listed successful businesses which started out or managed to stay afloat during depressions or economic crises called *The Obstacle Is the Way* by Ryan Holiday. I found it remarkable.

- Fortune Magazine – 90 days after the Market Crash of 1929
- FedEX – Oil Crisis 1973
- UPS – Panic of 1907

- Hewlett Packard – Great Depression, 1935
- Charles Schwab –Stock Market Crash of 1974-75
- Coors – Panic of 1873
- Costco – Recession in late 1970s
- Revlon – During the Great Depression, 1932

The reason for their success was the founders of these companies were all too busy living in the moment. Think about the difficulty perceived by so many people during those times. Yet, this list shows that not everyone thought the same. The list is longer as well.

So, if having Money is about our perception, what do you choose to see in this moment?

I hope you say Abundance!

How is it to live in a vibration of Abundance? It is knowing you are already there – a feeling of abundance, of joy, of freedom. It is the feeling of loving your work because you want to do it, not because you are dependent on work to survive. There is no room for lack, there is no scarcity. This belief is how I know *I am there*.

But here is the thing, even though I feel I am there, I also am aware that I am not done. It is not a place where I go and say, "Okay, I'm there. It's over."

It is a continued state of being. Therefore, Money keeps coming in.

I don't worry about spending or having enough. It seems the more I give, the more I get. It is not something I watch. I will check my bank account but not for fear of lack. I do it to enjoy the numbers. Financial abundance or success is not a goal or destination for me. It is an ongoing journey. And, oh my, what a fun one.

There was an instance where I had a card drawn for me by my good friend Rhonda at Intuitive Alchemy from Colette Baron Reid's deck. Keep in mind that I am in alignment with abundance and the feeling of joy and love. So, it was no surprise I received such a glowing card reading which resonated with me. It was a confirmation of where I was in that moment. The card read:

"You've entered a sweet time in your life enjoying the land of milk and honey that everyone wants to experience. It's an interlude that feels more languid than ambitious

*when all your senses are awake to
the unlimited possibilities in the
universe. These times are precious
and only come when you're in your
authentic zone wearing the world
as a loose garment, not wanting,
yet able to be nourished in ways
both tangible and subtle.
Abundance is an energy that you
are a living part of. All your needs
are being met. You are given the
gift of nourishment in every form.*

*There is only one authentic you.
This version of your Self is Spirit's
emissary in the world. When you're
in alignment with the truth you are
a unique expression of the Divine
your ago can rest and your soul can
illuminate your purpose. Now is
the time when you are seeking your
true north. When you find this
direction you automatically step
into prosperity and the world
brings you evidence of abundance.
Miracles are a choice and a way of
seeing the world. With every choice*

you make right now you have the
potential to seize good fortune and
embrace your destiny.
Opportunities will lead you to your
best life now. Be open to them.
You're getting a sweet taste of what
you want."

I believe every word in that card reading. Because the evidence is there when my clients come to me to manifest big Money. I mean BIG Money. And I love playing with this big energy of Money, even if it's just to get to a higher vibration. Every word of that card reading resonates with where I am now. It is my reality because I believe it.

And when you believe in yourself and in what you are doing, you, too, can master the Money mentality.

Prosperity, financial freedom, abundance, wealth, success or whatever word you want to call Money—it is simply an energy, a state of being, where you are always supported, and your needs are all provided for.

One of my favorite energy words for Money is "currency" because it feels delicious and delightful for me. Adopt a word which will bring that same sort of delight to your mind when you say it. Soon, you too will be getting a sweet taste of what you want. In this case, Money.

I want to share some of my personal favorite Prosperity Affirmations. Say each one aloud and feel the powerful energy of the words and how they make you feel. If at first you feel like you do not resonate with what you are saying, I encourage you to move towards it. The negative feeling is only the perception of fear and doubt keeping you from aligning yourself with the vibration of it. Keep repeating until you own it.

Change in mindset will occur in as much time as it takes for you to rewire your brain by changing your thoughts.

Prosperity Affirmations

I am a magnet for prosperity. It is drawn to me.
Prosperity and abundance come to me in expected and unexpected ways.
I am worthy of abundance and prosperity in my life.
I am open and receptive to all the wealth life offers me.
I embrace new avenues of prosperity and abundance.
I welcome an unlimited source of prosperity and wealth in my life.

I release all negative energy over
Money abundance and prosperity.
Money comes to me easily and
effortlessly.
I use my abundance and prosperity to
better my life and the lives of others.
My actions create constant prosperity.
I am aligned with the energy of
abundance.
I constantly attract opportunities which
create more abundance and prosperity.
My finances improve beyond my
dreams.
Money is the root of joy and comfort.
Money and spirituality can coexist in
harmony.
Money and love can be friends.

Let me just add that these affirmations are
worth billions.

Your thoughts are powerful.

What you focus on grows.

The stories you tell about yourself make a
difference.

Universe is listening to you.

Change your inner talk.

Be more self-aware and conscious about what you are thinking and saying about yourself.

Words carry a vibration.

So, if you want to become a thought billionaire, use some high energy words in the conversations you have with yourself.

Start adding words to your conversations such as such as gratitude, laughter, kindness, love, abundance, success, joy, freedom, power, enough, vision, glorious, light, overcomer, magic, empowered, strength, peace, limitless, awareness, collectiveness, constant, divine, fulfillment, force, honor, spiritual, certainty, sovereignty, splendid. (These words were given to me from a wonderful Goddess called Morrigan that I work with.)

Are they not the most amazing words? Enjoy the high vibration of them. I like to use them as affirmations, too. Such as, I AM Glorious.

When you reside in this vibration, Money situations you once thought only happened to "lucky" people will start happening to you. I like to call this Blue Money. I associate it with being the same kind of luck experienced by someone who hits the jackpot as someone who finds a dollar on the street or is given a coupon for Money off or even receiving a birthday gift. It comes out of the blue.

I have great story about Blue Money. I had not been anywhere in a while since I was enjoying coaching and helping others reach their potential. But an opportunity came up and I took it to go spend some time in Los Angeles with friends for my BFF's birthday.

My Blue Money started showing up as soon as I got to the airport. The airline asked for volunteers to change our seats to allow for some families to sit together. They gave each volunteer $125 just for complying. Not only that. I got moved up from the back of the plane to the front of the plane. It was sweet. At first it took me a second to realize, "Hey, that's Blue Money!

Then arriving into Los Angeles, I was picked up by friends. Yes, that is Blue Money too. The generosity of our friends always counts. I was also treated to dinner at some of Venice's finest restaurants.

After the first night at the hotel, my best friend and I came back from a happy day of shopping which included more discounts—30% off rain boots I had been wanting! The supervisor happened to be at the desk and asked how our stay was. I replied, "Okay." He said, "Just okay?" So, I told him we were here for my best friend's birthday and she wasn't quite pleased with the room and explained why. Next thing you know we were upgraded.

As we were settling into the new room, I was admiring the view and giving the hotel a positive review on our social media page when there was a knock on the door. It was champagne and desserts along with a Happy Birthday card to Candy. Very nice touch.

The entire time was so nice. We got to see friends, make good memories, and treated them for meals too. You know Money is energy, it just comes and goes. Flows in and out. I thought yes, this is the way we roll. Always something magical. I never did complain even when it came to the room conditions. All I did was tell the supervisor how it was because he asked. I know things will always work out for us. And did they ever!

Abundance is a state of mind.

It is fun realizing and appreciating being in a state of abundance and experiencing it firsthand.

The Universe conspires to give us what we want.

I live in a very abundant Universe. Trust that you can too, and you will master the Money mentality.

CH 4 ~ THE MONEY ALLERGY

Have you ever wondered where does your Money go? One day you have it, the next day it's gone. You could be signaling an allergy to Money. Being a pharmacist made me think of this one day. When I am doing consulting work it is my responsibility to check the patient's allergies right away.

In fact, if an allergy is not documented I cannot proceed with any drug recommendation for treatment. A notation of allergies must be documented even if it is NKA (no known allergy). Only then can I proceed with recommending and approving prescriptions.

Allergies can occur at any time in one's life. Allergies can come and go as well. Sometimes they stay. Then we just avoid the causing allergen. Sometimes the allergy is so severe that anaphylaxis could occur. The throat could close up! But what about an "allergy" to Money?

Money is not something we want to veer away from, rather it's best to treat the symptoms and keep Money in our company.

After taking part in countless Money Alchemy sessions, I started to notice a that some people seemed to have what resembled an allergy to Money. The signs, or symptoms, I identified were similar to what you might find when someone eats a food that is intolerable. It can also be akin to an allergy to pet dander or hay fever.

When you come across something which sets off an allergy you will naturally avoid the trigger. I'd like you to play along and see whether you might be suffering from a Money allergy and staying away from Money as a result.

The most common symptoms of a Money allergy can manifest as follows:

Thinking about Money makes you hesitate.
Talking about Money makes you uneasy.
Receiving Money makes you want to hide.

There is a constant struggle you have
with Money.
You have given up altogether on
Money.

Those allergies could trigger something
similar and as severe as anaphylaxis, but towards
Money!

Having an allergy to Money will make it
nearly impossible for you to consider having
Money get close to you again. That is **not** what
you want. In the same way that there are
medications to treat the symptoms of an allergy
and make it bearable, there are also ways to
relieve the ill at ease you feel coming on when
you encounter Money. As in allergy testing, you
start little by little—getting comfortable with
little amounts of Money coming in, even just
with small denominations.

I would like you to start by answering: Would
you be comfortable with 5 cents coming in? I
hope your answer is "Yes." Because if you could
appreciate receiving five cents and feeling
deserving of it, then increasing it to fifty cents, a
dollar, one hundred dollars, etc., you will slowly
but surely become immune to your Money
allergy.

After an alchemy session with a client, she
sent me an email explaining how she started

appreciating her five-cent nickel. She started feeling like it could be hers. She never felt she was deserving. She never felt Money could be hers. Her belief was that Money was for everyone else. It was not a possibility Money would enter her life. She thought this way her entire life up until appreciating this nickel. Then she noticed a shift. Money began to grow. Slowly at first, but Money started approaching her and eventually showing up a little bit more. She switched her perception and just like that, Money responded.

I want you to see Money as energy. Money is a vibration you tune into. After you become comfortable with small amounts of Money showing up, then you can start to feel worthy of having more of it. Appreciate every penny, nickel, dime, and dollar that comes in for you. Feel that Money belongs to you, and then some. Money loves abundance and so Money responds to the abundance of love and appreciation you give to it.

Abundance is a state of mind. Money and Abundance are two peas in a pod. Some people may find it easier to accept abundance in their lives because abundance can be seen and accepted in friendship, knowledge, food, health, or anything you accept as having much of. But there is nothing to stop you from having an abundance of Money, too. Visualize merging the two under one folder now in your mind. Money and Abundance cannot be separated any longer unless you remove the files. They are filed away together in your mind.

One day I played around with the idea of thinking of Money the way I think of my best friend. I gave Money the same traits I see in my BFF.

> Money doesn't judge me.
> Money loves me.
> Money always has my back.
> Money delights me.
> Money gives me gifts.
> Money is always happy to see me, and I am always happy to see Money.
> I sing to Money.
> I even kiss my Money (and I don't go around kissing just anyone!)

Nurture your Money just like you would your BFF.

Show your love and appreciation to Money.

What will Money do in return?

Just like a friend, it will show up more often.

It will want to be around you as much as you want to be around Money.

Money likes that vibration. Who doesn't like to feel loved and appreciated, right?

On my spiritual journey towards financial independence there was a time when getting to RELIEF and PEACE is all I focused on. It was the optimal vibration for me to focus on when there was a lot of contrast going on around me. By contrast I mean, lots of bills, putting food on the table, and making necessary purchases. I found that amping my vibe to relief and peace worked. That shift alone manifested MONEY.

Then something else remarkable happened. I remember feeling one day like a door had opened, or I got off an escalator. I remember it specifically happening in my brain. A shift had taken place.

I got to JOY.

I thought to myself, Oh my god, I got to joy. How did I do this?

Yes, peace and relief are awesome. They bring you to joy. Every now and again when I get knocked out of joy, I go to peace and relief and there I go headed into joy.

Money is attracted to joy, so Money follows your joy and comes in.

So next time you feel the sniffles coming on towards Money, think: relief, peace, and joy. That is your sweet spot.

Money and Joy are friends.

They are bed partners.

They are BFFs.

Get yourself to joy by talking to a good friend on the phone, going on a dog walk, smelling flowers. It doesn't have to be over the top. Joy is and can be everywhere. When you tune into joy, the neurons in our brain literally change. Even Google associates with this. Try Googling, "Change your brain" and you will have results suggesting, "Change your life."

Great teachers like the Buddha, Jesus, Moses, Mohammed, and Gandhi were all born with brains built essentially like ours—and then they changed their brains to serve from a mind that changed the world. Science is now revealing how the flow of thoughts sculpts the brain and we are learning it is possible to strengthen positive brain states. Think joy and Money and strengthen your immunity against ill feelings toward Money by changing how your brain reacts to Money.

Long ago I read something in the Bible when I was in high school which stuck with me. I may not remember it correctly so I'm not going to pretend to quote the Bible, but the moral of the story was ingrained into me. It was about a Jubilee where all debt was forgiven. I heard the word again many years later among spiritual (not religious) circles that a "Jubilee" was coming. Again, it was the idea that debt is forgiven, debt is paid, or literally debt be GONE!

When I heard this, it immediately brought back good thoughts. It brought an amazing delicious thought of, Wow, debt is gone. It feels so good. I don't owe anyone anything anymore. Could this be? No bills in the mail anymore? Wow, it feels so delightful. It feels liberating. It feels FREE. I continued to play with this thought. Each day I tuned into the vibration of having no debt.

I told myself it will be possible to be debt free. I also said one day these credit card companies are going to beg me to want their Money. These people are going to be throwing Money at me. They are going to want me to borrow their Money. They are going to ask me to have their Money. Although in 3D reality, I was in a deep hole of debt and the debt people were calling me on the phone trying to collect Money from me. But not in brain. In my brain, I was debt free. Jubilee!

I stayed steadfast in the belief that Jubilee existed. It existed for ME. In the heart of my heart I believed it would be true. I was always taught, and I quote my Money coach, "If you believe it, then it exists." I continued to tune into Jubilee. All I did was think about it. The way it would make me feel. Then it started to happen. As I look back, I realize that by tuning into the energy of Jubilee, I came into alignment with the energy of Jubilee, and all debt vanished. Literally.

Now it is true. Banks are trying to get me to borrow their Money and credit card companies have increased my line of credit. When I get those letters, I laugh. Envision, see yourself in a Jubilee where all your debt is taken care of. There is a place deep inside, in another state of mind where it exists for you, for everyone.

Another way of treating your allergy to Money is through dreaming. If you have ever dreamed of Money, you probably wondered what the dream meant. Does it mean Money is here? Is it coming? In my experience when I dream of Money it is a very positive and fun thing.

A few years ago, I dreamt Money four nights straight in a row. The word "retirement" came to me in my dream. At the time, it did not even seem remotely possible I could retire. It absolutely made no sense in my mind. Nonetheless, I wrote it down in my dream journal. Soon after I dreamt I saw $200,000, so I wrote it down in my journal, too.

Let me be clear that during this time when these dreams were occurring, I was in contrast.

Those two dreams felt so farfetched although, they gave me hope and brought me to relief and peace.

And getting to a place of relief and peace when you are feeling anxious about Money helps you make that little switch in your vibration which can align you back up with Money.

Dreaming about Money, I wake up happy with a renewed sense of awe inspiring hope. I might dream of actual green dollar bills or have the sensation of Money coming in. Some people say that I am so aligned with Money it makes sense I would dream about Money. I do believe Money shows up in our subconscious to help us heal a financial issue, or allergy to Money, but it also is a way for Money to communicate.

This is how it works. If Money shows up in your dreams, it is trying to connect with you. If the dream feels unpleasant towards Money, it is your subconscious picking up on the fears and doubts you have towards Money. Instead of feeling like you had a bad dream about Money when you wake up, send Money good thoughts for healing the connection.

Money needs you to repair the connection to it.

Imagine your Money allergy similar to when you are having a sneezing attack to pollen or itchy hives to dander. When you are feeling ill from an allergy you think about how all you want is to feel better. You see yourself in a healthy state and you want to get back to that state by any measure. That feeling of healthiness you are imagining, believe it or not, does send a message to your brain that could lessen the effects of the allergy by simply tuning into that healthy energy. You activate your own healing.

There is a definite energy to Money. It is such a powerful and consistent energy that I can feel how different it is to the energy of the metaphysical realm by comparison. I brought up in conversation with my friend Rhonda about what if we could put the energy of Money in a bottle? Her response was if I could channel Money's energy, which I could, then what would it feel or smell like? Would it be a flower essence or a sweet liquid? Wow, it was a powerful suggestion.

I would like you to play with that idea. It can be anything that comes to you when you tune into Money. If it's liquid or vapor or sugar crystals, whatever it is, put it into a bottle, like a magic potion, and take it in doses whenever you feel the allergy coming on. For me it was healing stones, which I had made with the word

"Money" on them. Feeling the stones in my hand creates a shift in energy. For my clients they are healing stones which reconnects them to the energy source of Money.

I want you to feel the certainty of Money and totally trust it is coming.

It is your birthright to feel you are worthy of this Money.

Sit with Money and feel good with it.

Now, imagine how good it would feel for the perfect amount of Money to show up for you. If you still can't, take the little bottle with the magic potion and drink up. It's time to get rid of your Money allergy.

CH 5 ~ MANIFESTING MONEY

There is a game I like to play called *Manifesting $1000 in 10 Days*. It was taught to me by my Money coach. It's totally doable, it's fun, it's easy. And I have played it many times over. There are times I play just to reinforce my manifesting ability. Then one day, I toyed with the idea to up the ante. My Money coach was telling me she was going to start a 30-day scripting workshop to manifest ten thousand dollars. I said, "What? Oh, I want in on that." I had never intentionally manifested $10,000. This was going to be fun, especially as a group venture. I could hardly wait to get started.

I set the intention.

I let it go.

Within a couple of days, I was already up a few thousand dollars. It was so awesome. I laughed with delight and said to myself with a chuckle, *Okay, only $8,000 more to go.*

Thoughts become things

When I woke up the next morning, I had manifested $11,000 in just twenty-four hours! I not only hit goal, I surpassed it.

When I went back to ask my Money coach when our 30 days would be officially up, she said she didn't know exactly. We had both forgotten to set the finish line because we simply set the intention and went on about our business. It was then when I realized that this game thrives on being light and loose. No tightness, no striving. Literally it is ALL FOR FUN.

When you let go of attachment, you let the magic in. Set an intention and then just let it go. Let it be easy. Let it be light. Let it be fun. The energy of Money is just that—FUN.

Some common questions I receive are: How do I manifest what I want? Why does it not seem to come fast enough? Can I change that?

My answer: It's all about vibration and alignment.

When you take a shot at manifesting, what else are you thinking in addition to what you want? Are you attaching negative or doubtful thoughts? Remember, your thoughts have power. What you focus on grows. If you focus on what you don't have, you get exactly that—what you don't have.

Perhaps you are attaching worry. Impatience. Distrust. Maybe fear. These thoughts all send a signal to the Universe that you are not trusting. But, if you are aligned in joy then all the good things that are aligned with your highest desires start happening spontaneously. When you are aligned in your worthiness and self-love that is when all you want to manifest comes in.

Life is meant to be fun. Life is meant to be joyful.

Allow the Universe to do its magic.

If you are intervening all the time, Universe cannot do its magic.

It takes practice. It requires consistency.

You cannot do your alignment work for a few days and then stop. It does not work that way. I have been practicing, speaking, and writing affirmations for over five years now. Louise Hay made her empire with affirmations. I don't miss a day. At first, I had to make reminders to myself. I set intentions to remember. I'm not saying this is going to take you five years because it did not take me that long. It is simply the time I've spent doing this now.

Time is fleeting, and all you need to do is keep practicing until it becomes a habit or a routine.

My tip is for you is to create a regular alignment practice. It takes just five minutes a day. Eventually, you can increase the time. Start with less time if you need to, but just focus on what you want to manifest with joy, love, fun, self-worth.

You can do this, I know you can. I'm cheering for you.

One New Year's Eve, just for fun, a friend suggested we make a list of things we wanted to experience or learn. This was different to me than my customary intention list I was used to writing which consists of some serious things I want to manifest in the year. This list my friend was suggesting was just for some lighthearted fun. I thought to myself, *Okay, how about flying?* At first, it seemed completely impossible to me—even though I have had a couple of dreams of me flying, but those didn't count for this exercise.

My intention was to *feel* the sensation of flying.

Shortly thereafter, one night as I was sleeping, I dreamt of being in the air with nothing below me —I often astral travel, so I know the difference between dreaming and traveling—then I began to fall in the air. I remember the exhilaration and the butterflies in my stomach. I could only compare it to a scene out of the *Matrix* where Neo jumps off the building. It felt like several minutes of me flying and falling. The best part is when I heard the phrase "going down your list." It was a big amazing WOW for me.

When shifts in my life take place to show me something I never would have thought possible, I think to myself, *In a million years, I would have never thought this would happen*. For instance, like becoming the Money Alchemist. If anyone would have told me a year ago that I would be a Money alchemist today, I would have said, *Get out of here*. My list of the things that are improbable or impossible are showing up and becoming POSSIBLE.

I realize Money is just like that, too. It seems impossible to be able to align up to the energy of Money, but it really is possible.

Money can come to you like metal to magnet.

When you realize you have achieved something you never thought possible, it makes you wonder what more "impossible" experiences you can achieve. Whatever those experiences are, tell yourself, you *can* ask for what you think is not possible.

There is no limit. The possibilities are endless.

I was deeply inspired by one of my clients who I worked with for three months. Her request was, "Ming, take me to the Moon." Well, with a request like that only magic would ensue. I was sure of it. She said her affirmations and her I AM Worthy statements. She counted her blue dollars while playing $1,000 in 10 days—she saw them to turn into green dollars. She made sure she was in alignment before sending out any emails or filling out an application. Every response returned to her was pure magic.

On our last coaching call, she shared with me she what felt and how she could SEE herself for the first time on the Red Carpet at the Oscars. As we went through her visualization, she had made her movies, she had her interviews, and she was now accepting her Oscar. In fact, as she was sharing what she was SEEING, what she was FEELING, I could feel and see it, too. It was that powerful. The energy of it was palpable. I could barely say anything to her besides, "Right on!" (and laughing with delight). We both agreed, she was already a winner. We were circling the moon and back. Right there, that is the perfect example of the power of visualization.

Manifesting Money is about alignment and belief.

To manifest what we desire, what we want, we need to put a little focus on what feels delicious. Because when we are feeling good and exhilarated, we are drawing in what we want to feel good and exhilarated about.

Our relationship to Money is meant to be fun; it is meant to have a great, incredible life with.

I was sitting with the energy of Money in my meditation when an invocation or activation came in. I was told to share it with you.

> I allow Money in to my life. I allow Money in my mail box. I allow Money into my bank account. I allow Money into my purse and wallet. I allow Money to flow effortlessly and easily to me. I welcome Money to blanket me with its certainty. I welcome Money because I am worthy. Money comes from the north, the south, the east and the west.

Money comes from all places unseen.
There is no fear where Money is.
Money is happy. Money is free. Money
is certain. Money is glorious. Money
delights me. Money is magic. Money
loves to multiply. Money loves to give.
Money loves to receive. Money is
balance. Money is love. I choose to
align myself with Money. And so it is.

To create the things or experiences we want, we just need to spend a few moments in the day spending some time imagining what we want, but never have had before...and let it get delicious. Let that feeling build and then let it go. By letting go you are releasing the attachment part.

You just need to let it go.

Then go have fun doing whatever you love to do.

One day I thought it would be nice to have a credit card with points. Though, when I was in contrast years ago, I had closed my credit card accounts. I was even told I was not going to be able to get them back. But on this occasion, I thought about how delicious it would be to have a card which gave me points because I was contemplating taking a trip. As I was browsing the airline website, I saw a button to apply for a credit card. I smiled and thought, *What the heck, might as well try*. Never say never.

The confirmation said I would receive a text message if I was approved. There was no text that night, but by bedtime I had forgotten all about it. I went to bed. The next morning, I woke up to an email approving my credit application...and by the end of the night, right in the middle of dinner, my credit card was Fed Ex'd to me. Who says we can't manifest what we want? There is no secret to manifesting Money. It is a magic we all possess. It is an ability we all have, to be able to ask and so receive.

I get asked a lot about my affirmations. People want to know what my affirmations are and do I change them up. When the question first came up, I took time to consider my reply. I was in my fifth straight year of reciting affirmations. The reason I enjoy them so much is because they are not only effective, they are so easily accomplished. I'm all about making it easy.

Again, going back several years when I was in deep contrast, I couldn't even think of my own affirmations, so I adopted them from my Money coach. They were:

Joy, Delight, and Satisfaction.

I recited those three simple but powerful words every day.

At the time, I'm not even sure I even said, "I AM joy, delight, and satisfaction." I believe I just tuned into the thought of everything bringing me just that. Even though I may not have been feeling joy, delight, and satisfaction when I was reciting them, it still came because I affirmed it. Delight and satisfaction came within my situation, even if I had to wait a day or two, but it came.

There were times when I couldn't tune into joy and I would substitute the affirmation with peace.

"I am peace."

All I wanted was peace in the place of so much turmoil around me. I am also born in the year of the rabbit (Chinese zodiac)—the rabbit seeks and needs peace. If I don't have peace it is difficult for me to move, period. But peace came over me and the situations around me. As time went on, and I described this to you before, joy popped up. I realized I had shifted to joy because I could feel it. This is where I like to remain. In JOY. Pretty much 24/7. I love the vibration of joy and it suits me well.

Now that I am in a much higher vibration and I have learned some words from the Goddesses, these are my affirmations currently:

I AM enough.
I AM glorious.
I AM Money.

And, yes, borrowing others' affirmations is okay. It worked for me.

I had this little ah ha moment one morning as I was preparing for a client call. I was all lit up on changing the brain. It came to me as a reminder that when we change our inner talk we become more self-aware.

The word "NOW" came to mind.

Using the word NOW is like pressing the "ENTER" button on the key board. And it felt powerful.

As I sat with this new perception, it entered my mind that this awareness was like telling our conscious mind to do the action NOW. So, I put my new word with my I AM affirmations:

NOW, I AM a rocking Money Alchemist.
NOW, I AM a wealthy philanthropist.
NOW, I AM assisting on raising the vibration of the planet.
NOW, I AM partnering up with the most amazing people on the planet.

NOW, I AM assisting animals all over the planet.

NOW, I AM doing my heart's delight work.

NOW, I AM doing life altering work.

NOW, I AM shifting people's vibration, so they can manifest their heart's desires.

Or use it with high energy words:

NOW, I AM in gratitude.

NOW, I AM in love.

NOW, I AM in abundance.

NOW, I AM in joy.

NOW, I AM in good health.

NOW, I AM in laughter.

NOW, I AM in kindness.

NOW, I AM in freedom.

Wow, how good did that feel? It feels powerful to me. Play with this and see how it feels for you. Happy manifesting!

CH 6 ~ FINANCIAL MAGIC

When I play with Money there is always Magic. I believe in Magic and if you are reading this, more than likely, so do you. Inspired by the book *Financial Sorcery* by Jason Miller, I'd like to share a few things I enjoyed from the book which resonated with me:

> *"If we cannot serve Money and we cannot avoid Money, that really leaves one option: to master it."*

I love this statement because it is true; we do not want to serve Money, we also cannot avoid it. Therefore, why not master it, why not understand it—why not love it?

Another quote I love:

"We have creativity and genius and strength of spirit. There is no longer a well-trod path for living a prosperous and happy life. Today we must make our own path, and magical people are good at that."

To create a magical connection with Money energy, I want you to feel the "certainty" of Money. That you totally TRUST not only because it is making its way to you, it is your birthright.

Feel your worthiness of this Money and your magical connection to it.

By restricting your use of magic or treating magic as something to be used as a last resort to manifest Money, you are almost guaranteeing that you will not be very skilled in the use of magic.

Think about it. How do you get good at something?

Practice.

This is a word I say repeatedly to my clients. Practice. Practice. Practice.

Practice your alignment.

Practice tuning into your vibration.

Practice self-love.

Practice receiving.

Practice showing love and appreciation to the Money that is coming in.

Keep practicing. The more you practice, the easier it becomes. And Money will always be there for you, magically.

Earlier, I spoke about creating Money stones for my clients. When I connected to the energy of Money, I was able to channel what form it would take so that I could always carry it with me. It came to me as a stone—a Magical Money Stone.

These Money stones are so highly attuned to the vibration of Money and amplified with Reiki and Goddess Energy. I passed them out to my clients and group members. The stones are so magical, some of them "sing" to my clients. I have even had reports that they move around! I have received numerous testimonies of how these stones have created Money miracles in the lives of my clients.

The magic appears through other channels as well. During the time I was going through some very serious contrast, I practiced keeping my vibration at the highest place possible. I was very clear this was going to be key for my survival. I kept a tight circle of friends whom I definitely knew would support me and would not bring my vibe down. I kept my thoughts in check on a regular basis. Each time a thought of anxiety or fear came in, I dialed off it. But it wasn't just my vibration that was assisting me, I had higher power help from my Magical Divine Team.

My divine team consists of Archangels, angels, fairies, spirit animals, goddesses, dragons, and even the Pleiadeans and Kryon. Magic works with nature, is part of nature, and as such is subject to the same ethics and considerations as any other type of action. And my Magical Divine Team reminds me that EVERYTHING is vibration.

We live in a vibrational Universe.

Everything has energy.

In working with metaphysical energy and Money energy, I recognize that the energy of Money is different than that of my divine team. In connecting to each of them, I feel the palpable difference. What they all have in common is that each and every single entity has been involved in supporting and helping me raise my vibration to the intention of abundance.

When I started seeking abundance, angels were always near me, so it was natural I brought them on board to help with the contrast I was facing. I called on Archangel Nathaniel and asked for his divine help since his team likes a challenge. Then one day, fairies came in. Yes, they were Money fairies. In fact, they were MY very own Money Fairies. At that time, I had never even heard of fairies on a metaphysical basis. I didn't know they actually existed in our earthly realm. Until I heard them. Now I see them regularly showing up for me.

I set an intention for my Money fairies to be fun, amazing, and healing. What do they go and do? They delivered, and they delivered FAST. They were faster than angels! Because they are elementals, they are able to help quickly. I named them Ming's Money Fairies. They are so amazing. The amazing thing about them is they are generous. I love that about them. I can send them to my friends who need a boost of magic, and I watch the magic happen.

Fairies love to be chatted to and talked about. I've had group calls where I include the fairies and talk about them and the fairies will continue to play with all those who call on them. I also meditate with them. The fairies told me about a big project they wanted to help me work on. They giggled in delight as I replied without hesitation, "Okay let's do it." The wonderful thing is that as far as Money goes, I could sense from the fairies that Money is never going to be an issue for me ever again.

Now that you are familiar with Ming's Money Fairies, you, too, can call on them. Know for certain these Money fairies are extremely generous in assisting with your abundance.

All you need to do is believe and receive.

The fairies will joyously come to your aid when you ask for their help.

Then there are Dragons. The magic with dragons started with one green dragon named Doremus who appeared to me during the time I was in great contrast. It was during the same time in my life where I was having to manifest Money to pay my mortgage, feed my dogs and myself, pay my bills, etc. So, having a dragon around was awesome. He could do all things you imagine a dragon can do. However, he was also a healer. He assisted in our Reiki Fur Babies work as well.

It's been a very magical journey and relationship with Doremus. I call him my lead dragon and his energy is always around me; he stays close and appears if I need him. The other three dragons came later. They are Maximus, Cornelius, and Belrique (red, yellow, and blue, respectively). I have a new one, too. He's gold and purple. I almost have his name. I'm sure it will soon come to me. These dragons assist me in other vibrational healing work as well. But the dragons' connection to me with Money is what is astounding. This is how the magic came together.

As I mentioned before, my clients along with everyone in our group received a Money stone from me. These green Aventurine stones, being a natural abundance stone, were also amplified by Reiki and Goddess energy to give them an extra boost. I have been told many amazing testimonies about Money magically coming in for people when they received their stones. Remember I mentioned they move around. The stones do like to travel. I have heard about them flying on planes, going on trips and business meetings, creating magical circumstances with Money.

Anyway, long story short, I started binge watching *Game of Thrones*. Now, one guess, which character did I fall in love with? In fact, my friends and family have told me for years to watch this show just for this character—the Mother of Dragons. As I started watching, I could not get enough of this character. The dragons entered my vortex even more, and my own dragons became closer than ever.

Here's where the Money stone and dragon come in. It was synchronicity as its best. I started reading *Mystical Dragon Magick* by DJ Conway.

Something told me to read the second book first. As I started section one, it talked about stones that are of use to the apprentice. My jaw dropped as I read:

"Green aventurine attracts unexpected adventures, something every Apprentice should expect. Dragons delight in revealing the unexpected. It is also a prosperity and good fortune stone."

When I read this, I was so excited realizing that I have been surrounding myself with these Money stones. They started to feel like dragon eggs to me. What synchronicity—Magical Money Stones are in fact dragon stones!

This is the most incredible part of my journey so far: the magic that has been revealed to me by my metaphysical divine team.

This is also proof, again, to follow who you are. You never know how the journey will unfold.

As I mentioned earlier, my journey began with asking Archangel Nathaniel for help, but I also call on Archangel Michael, Archangel Raphael, Archangel Chamuel, Archangel Jophiel, Archangel Gabriel, Archangel Uriel and Archangel Zadkiel. I know they have the ability to be everywhere and anywhere at any time. There is no time issue with them and they will assist anyone who asks for intervention.

They all want to help us, but human beings have free will, we need to ask.

Archangels have been working with me for years with energy healing for the animals and the planet, so it only made sense they showed up to amplify and align my vibration to Money.

The angels want us to be abundant.

They fully support us in making our lives easier. They want us to expand and to make more choices for our highest good. It is important to CHOOSE and choose often the experience we want to have.

A choice you make is an intention you set.

The angels can help you once you make a choice to make life easier by asking them for faith to believe this is true even when you are not feeling it. Ask the angels for their help in releasing anything which is not serving you.

If it's a big challenge, remember Archangel Nathaniel is always up for the task.

My spirit animals are Bo the lion, Jade the black panther, Jedi the white tiger, Malmas the dolphin, Kennai the fox, Bodhisattva the white horse, King the Pitbull, and Kauai the brown bear. Also, on my team are my transitioned animals, Sammy Diva my yellow lab and Mochi my Maine Coon to name a couple.

This entire team of spirit animals will assist you as well, on any level. They are all so very generous, too.

I'm happy to share my team with you—the only requirement is you must call on them and ask for help.

But there's more. Just as the Archangels and angels want us to be abundant and support our connection with Money, Kryon appreciates Money and wants human beings to appreciate Money as well. So much, that he has given us an equation to tap into for attracting Money, aligning up with the energy of Money and bringing it literally into your vortex.

I've mentioned "certainty" within these pages several times. When I started doing Money alchemy, I was given a word whenever I tuned into the energy of Money. That word is CERTAINTY.

Each time I tuned into the energy of Money, I could feel the certainty.

It was powerful.

It felt exactly like that, *certain*.

Certain I knew Money was coming. Certain I would always be okay. Certain there would never be any lack. Certain I would always be cared for.

It so happened during my meditation practice and vibrating with "certainty" that I came into connection with Kryon who gave me the EQUATION to Money. I was like, "EUREKA!!!" I was so excited, and it made SO MUCH SENSE to me.

Here it is:

WORTHINESS = UNCONDITIONAL LOVE = ENERGY = MONEY

I saw this equation in a black box with a heart on it.

Certainty is the energy of Money. How do you get there?

Look at the equation again. You must feel worthy.

Best way to feel worthy is to do I AM WORTHY statements like: I am worthy of love, I am worthy of Money, I am worthy of joy and so on.

When you see your Self, and love your Self, and allow unconditional love toward your Self, you line your Self up to the energy of Money.

I invite you to play with this equation. Tap into what is certain by thinking about what is certain to you. It could be your fur baby's unconditional love, or the sun setting and rising, or water flowing downhill.

When you tap into what is certain, right there is the energy of Money.

It is always CERTAIN.

One more thing about dragons I discovered in the book *Mystical Dragon Magick*, DJ Conway wrote, and I quote:

> *"What we little realize is that we make a daily impact on our own lives by the kinds of thoughts we constantly hold and dwell on. Like attracts like, remember? If you are constantly pessimistic, believe you are a pawn in life, don't think you deserve or never will have good luck and a changed and better future, then you certainly will get what your thoughts send out daily on the energy waves of the Multiverse.*
>
> *You must learn to visualize the positive result you want as an accomplished task. You must speak*

of it in the same manner. Don't
say, "I want to find a soul mate."
Rather, word it as a completed goal:
" I thank you dragons, for bringing
me my soul mate to me."

Remember you have Dragons on your side, as well as an exhaustive metaphysical Magical Divine Team. It is incredible how everything which connects us to Money fits together and connects through all these different metaphysical channels and beings.

We call it magic because the workings behind the scenes which brings us Money, are not apparent.

We cannot see the energy. We can only feel energy. But what we can see is the conspiring and coming together of events, of people, of situations taking place to bring us the abundance, the blue Money, the savings, the new car, the Money...as if by magic.

CH 7 ~ LOVE AND MONEY

Self-love is the KEY to manifesting anything. It really is. The year 2016, I finally got there. Ever since then, I have been practicing self-love fully—all the way.

How did I realize this? Because I downloaded this affirmation:

I AM Enough.

The day this affirmation was given to me, I felt it all the way through the core of my heart. It resonated with me completely and fully. I felt peace like I had never felt before. I felt happiness like I had never felt before. It arrived on Christmas day of 2016. And it was the most amazing gift I could give myself.

If you truly feel you are enough, you will lack nothing. All is taken care of. It is an amazing vibration to live in, to resonate with. Practice tapping into it. You'll know when you are there; similarly, you'll know when you are not. Which is why CERTAINTY became a very important word for me. Not just because it is the vibration of Money, but also because Certainty is part of the equation along with Unconditional Love which is where self-love abides, too.

Being raised in a family where Money was often a measure of love could sometimes make it difficult to appreciate Money. In fact, it made me not like Money so much. Giving Money to each other was a measure of love and it became sort of a superficial replacement to saying, "I love you" to one another. It was a phrase that was not said much in my family.

All that has changed now, though. However, it took several years of showing my parents how saying the words "I love you" was worth a lot of Money. Now, when Money is shared between family members the love is profoundly felt because it is no longer a means for showing love, it is an energy we love to share with one another.

As I am doing Money alchemy sessions with clients, what often comes up is how their relationship with Money is related to how they feel about themselves. Self-love and worthiness is such an integral part of manifesting Money. As you know Money is energy, and when you flow love and appreciation towards Money as it comes to you, Money enjoys that and flows to you more.

But can you hold onto that Money?

Many of us, myself included at one time, think we need to work hard for Money. We need to earn our Money, we need to struggle and work for every penny that comes in. But the Money doesn't seem to want to stick around, so we work harder. But, let me tell you how I know you do not need to work hard to make Money.

You are not making Money. You are attracting Money to you.

There are times when I am talking to a client when I will not even mention Money with them. I know they want to manifest Money, otherwise they wouldn't hire me as their Money coach. But, some sessions are focused primarily on the practice of self-love for thirty days. It may sound like a difficult task to practice self-love for an entire month, especially when you are not used to it.

You may ask yourself: How do I do that? Where do I begin?

It's a practice and I would ask that you start by simply writing out I AM Worthy statements.

And, as you do these self-love practices, you will notice an internal shift occurring within you. The first thing you may come to realize is that there is some lack of loving yourself. But, as you connect with your internal self and present more and more love to yourself with affirmations and statements and self-talk, Money starts sticking around.

There is a definite correlation between self-love and Money. You may even get an ah ha moment. You will realize, "If I love myself more, I will not only feel I am worthy of receiving Money and love, I will know it.

Believe it.

Play with it.

You will find that connection.

You only need to think about your self-love and worthiness; don't even think about your need or want for Money. Take note of how it goes. Keep a journal or a log where you can write down how you are feeling, what you are practicing and any thoughts which come to you. It is the best way to notice when a shift is happening.

Money is related to how you feel about yourself. As explained to you before, the equation of Money is: Worthiness = Unconditional Love = Energy = Money. How you feel towards you is an integral piece in manifesting Money. In flowing with the energy of love and appreciation towards your Self, Money makes its way to you, because you know Money is energy vibrating to the same tune of Love.

If on the other hand, you are a feeling a little less than fabulous about yourself, it is not a problem.

Pour on the self-love like your finest fragrance.

Shower yourself with self-love as though you are under a waterfall.

When you pour on the self-love it causes a reset, like rebooting your internal processor. You clear out all the junk, switch off, and restart. This shift is about reconnecting to your inner being and who you are deep down.

So, take a deep breath right now.

Breathe out slowly.

Ah, that is the beginning of self-love right there…in that breath.

I encourage you to start a self-love ritual. Perhaps in the morning, a few minutes before bed, or at lunch just be with yourself. Get centered, take some deep breaths, maybe a short meditation, and take a few moments to say some affirmations or take a few seconds with some gratitude focusing on what is going right.

There is always something right, even amid chaos; you just need to notice it. In the beginning, you might have to look for it if you are in contrast. But just the smallest token of good, of something going right, is enough to be grateful.

Here are a few tips on showing self-love towards yourself and finding something positive and right.

- Self-love can be as easy as anything that makes you smile.
- Self-love is filling your body with nourishing food and drink.
- Self-love is loving that beautiful body of yours.
- Self-love is surrounding yourself with people who love and encourage you.
- Self-love is realizing there is only ONE of you on this planet. You are unique and truly a gift.
- Self-love is celebrating all your wins.
- Self-love is following your passion.

- Self-love is always evolving so be kind and support yourself when you are going through some tough times.
- Self-love is forgiving yourself for that one thing you did which made you feel bad or guilty—it is time to let it go.
- Self-love is doing things which light you up such as painting, singing, hiking, dancing, cooking, whatever it is that elevates your spirit and feels good to your soul.

The other thing I encourage you to see is Money and Love can be friends.

I really want to emphasize this to you.

Money and love can be friends.

I have thought about this phrase so much and it means several things to me. Your first thought from reading this book so far might be that the connection between a Money and Love friendship is self-love. It certainly is because it is all related to the equation of Money. It does have to do with self-love, for sure. However, it is also about the love in your relationships.

During some of Money alchemy sessions, a few of them turned into relationship coaching.

Some of my clients began having shifts in their relationships. I never thought of myself as a relationship coach either. But it became apparent that relationships are very much related to Money.

Money and Love must go hand in hand.

In fact, when I manifested my own boyfriend, I had written out this intention:

> I have a guy who sees "me" for who I am, what I love, and I what I want to create in this Universe. He sees animals the way I do, as important and equal beings. He likes me, we have a strong friendship. He loves me and has eyes only for me. He's trustworthy, kind, funny, and makes me laugh. We also have a strong chemistry. We both can do magical things. When we are not together, it is okay. We both support each other in whatever it is that we are doing.

This was a powerful intention because all of it came true. Phillip is exactly ALL these things. Phillip is also good with Money. In fact, he was so much better with Money than I was years ago. He helped me see the energy of Money. This realization became an important concept to Money alchemy as much as self-love.

When you align your energy up to Money, Love comes.

When you get your energy aligned up to Love, Money comes.

Because Money and Love can be friends.

You will notice for yourself, when you are in a good relationship with yourself, you are aligned with Money. But have you noticed when you are in a good relationship with your husband, wife, partner, girlfriend, boyfriend, you are also aligned with Money? If you haven't, I ask you to look at your relationships, past, present or future, and notice the correlation between them and Money.

When you are in a good relationship, there is always abundance. Or the feeling of abundance. And totally the opposite when you are not in a good relationship. Even if you have a lot of Money in your account, you will not feel abundant because of the attachment to a poor relationship. See the connection?

Now is a good time to bring up worthiness again because when you feel worthy of a good relationship, you attract a partner who is worthy of you. If you do not feel you are worthy of someone good, even if they are, you will not feel your partner is the right one. There will be contrast and conflict because you are not feeling worthy. Same with Money. If you don't feel worthy of Money, even when you have it, you will feel you do not have enough.

One of the best ways to get into the worthiness vibration is literally by reciting I AM Worthy statements. It is a very powerful practice and will literally bring in miracles.

How so?

Because your vibration is everything. If we are vibrating worthiness all sorts of good stuff come to. Even if you feel like you are already pretty good at doing this, there is no limit. You can still amp up your worthiness with these statements. They are enriching, and empowering, and shift producing.

This practice is how my Money Alchemist web page came into existence. I was writing these I AM Worthy Statements in my journal every day. Immediately after I wrote my I AM Worthy statements the first time, I got a download of intuition on what the content of this website would be. I must stress this was a big deal because it is not my highest joy to create websites. So, when the inspiration hit, I was amazed.

I AM Worthy statements are very powerful for amping self-love and discovering for yourself that connection between Love and Money.

I AM Worthy of LOVE.
I AM Worthy of MONEY.
I AM Worthy of ABUNDANCE.
I AM Worthy of good HEALTH.
I AM Worthy of HAPPINESS.
I AM Worthy of the PERFECT CLIENTS.
I AM Worthy of HEALTHY and HAPPY ANIMALS.
I AM Worthy of a LOVING FAMILY.
I AM Worthy of a FANTASTIC HOME.
I AM Worthy of AMAZING FRIENDSHIPS.
I AM Worthy of JOY.
I AM Worthy of the PERFECT PARTNERSHIPS.
I AM Worthy of an EASY LIFE.

You get the drift. Try it and watch the shifts which will take place as you connect with high vibration of these statements.

I had another moment of realization when I started writing a blog post one day and gave it the title: "Journey to Love." But then instantly I realized I am already *at* Love and I am on a *continuing* journey of love! And, so, I changed the title. I thought back on that one Christmas when I had the realization of total self-love, that I am enough. That feeling, that awareness, was the biggest gift I had ever given to myself. It was such a sense of freedom and of joy.

It truly is a gift when you can love and enjoy your own company!

My awareness of love is that love is the highest vibration on the planet. Love exists for all mankind and exists as an energy, a vibration every human being can focus on—be it self-love, love to our friends, love to our family, love to our pets, love to our fellow man. When we focus on the love, we raise the vibration of the planet.

This is true since wherever two people are gathered in love, the collectiveness of the love is so much more powerful.

I was talking to a good friend during lunch one day on the subject of romantic love without sex. She asked me if I could have sex without love. I said, "Absolutely." Then she suggested if that were true, I could have romantic love without sex. For me, this idea was profound. Mulling it over, though...maybe there was more to it I needed to explore.

I recalled one of my core values is CONNECTION. Connection is an extremely important value to me. When I lose connection, things don't feel right. People close to me know this. I may not have a lot of close friends, but the ones who are know that connection is paramount to me.

Then I thought about all the different languages of love. Love languages for me are: gift giving, quality time, words of affirmation, acts of service (devotion), and physical touch. Not everyone embraces or 'speaks' all the languages to have love, just like we do not speak every language in the world to understand one another. Which led me to view sex, physical touch, connection, as a language of love.

So, you can see where my conclusion landed. From my perspective, human beings experience the languages of love differently. But all forms of Love are acceptable.

I resonate with this centuries-old definition, if you will, of love:

> *"Love is patient, love is kind. It does not envy, it does not boast, it is not proud. It does not dishonor others, it is not self-seeking, it is not easily angered, it keeps no record of wrongs. Love does not delight in evil but rejoices with the truth. It always protects, always*

trusts, always hopes, always
perseveres."

If you are still asking, "What does love have to do with Money?"

Let me just say, "Oh everything!!"

Remember, it's in the equation of Money: Worthiness= Unconditional Love= Energy= Money.

The Beatles sang it best, *All You Need is Love.* Thanks to me, you will probably be hearing that song in your head now because I do, too. Ha! But I really believe this to be truer than true. Yes, we hear phrases like, *Love makes the world go 'round, Love is this…and Love is that…*

I am one who talks about self-love A LOT. In just about every page you have read so far you know I also teach that self-love and unconditional love are directly related to our Money flow.

But I want to end this chapter by discussing the love we have for each other, for the ones we love. And for the ones we do not feel lovable towards—the ones whom we are angry with or the ones who have disappointed us in some way, shape or form. It feels easier to be in the place where you don't think you need them or you don't miss them at all.

But when you come around full circle to Love, Love is so much more powerful, so encompassing, so everlasting and so deep and meaningful. It is a vibration that gives you the sensation of coming home—a familiar space of warmth, light, beauty. And everything that surrounds you, surrounds you with the familiar feeling of pure Love.

It is much easier to Love than it is to be antipathy.

It requires more energy to focus on the opposite of Love. And when you are full circle in Love, it transcends any lower vibrations you were attached to. You become a source of Love.

Abraham Hicks says:

*"Absence of love is painful.
Emotion of love is an indicator of
alignment."*

Apply it to any subject or any relationship. No matter what it is, the emotional scale on end feels like love is your freedom and empowerment perception. How you perceive something is tied to the feeling of alignment. In most relationships, especially in the beginning of one, both people are more in alignment because you are looking positively. Finding the best in each other. What that is, is aligning to Source.

When you love, you are in alignment.

Once again, I repeat, Love has everything to do with our energetic alignment. No wonder it feels so good to be doing what I do. When I do the practice, I feel the circumference of love. (And what do you know, as I'm writing on this occasion I receive an unexpected check for $200 for no reason—out of the blue.) There must be a link.

Stay in the Love.

Let us spread the Love.

Where there is Love there is Money.

Now watch Money come rolling in.

CH 8 ~ GIVING AND RECEIVING

Giving and receiving is a HUGE part of increasing our abundance. Like myself, you probably do not have any trouble with giving. I have spoken to lots of people who say they love to give whether it is a birthday gift, a lunch, a coffee, or Money even. It feels good to give to someone especially when it's something they have wanted or needed.

It's not surprising how many people, myself included, thought I was a good receiver, too. I am now, but this wasn't always the case. Receiving was a huge lesson I had to learn, and every time I tell people my story on how it happened, it resonates with them. Because I've learned that receiving is a lot harder to do than giving.

Several years ago, I had a birthday approaching. It was my first birthday after separating from my ex-husband. My little brother suggested I practice my receiving muscle by having a birthday party. Funnily, I never had the experience of one before.

Naturally, one would imagine that the thought of me throwing a birthday party for myself would make me happy.

No, it did not.

In fact, I cried myself to sleep that night thinking about it, wondering if anyone would even come. Did I have any friends? Absurd thinking for sure, but the thought of having a birthday party simply terrified me.

As I've mentioned before, there is a part of me who prefers to move through fear. And who besides me knows me better than anyone else— my BFF Candy. She actually gave me a big birthday party that year. And lots of people showed up. Not only was I blown away by the entire experience with the wonderful gifts or the delicious food or the delightful wine.

An amazing thing happened.

It was when my little brother sat beside me and told me publicly *why* he loved me. Then everybody, one by one took turns doing the same. Talk about having to practice receiving. There were tears everywhere.

After that moment, I had a profound internal shift within me which helped me learn to receive without hesitation. And, as I continued practicing receiving, Money kept POURING in.

This is when I realized giving and receiving had to be in *balance*.

Shortly after my moment of realization on receiving, I had an opportunity to put it into practice. I received several gift certificates to get a facial, so reluctantly I decided to go. Now you may think, oh wow, a facial—how fun. No, not for me. It felt like "work" to me." But, I needed to turn that belief around if I was going to receive the gift of the wonderful facials.

I laid down on the table, the aesthetician asked me to take several deep breaths, and as I did, I set the intention to RECEIVE the healing and wonderful facial. What I perceived as an unpleasant effort turned into a relaxing and soothing facial treatment. Now I love facials. What a shift. Although it does take practice!

Remember I gave you my analogy on merging the Abundance folder with the Money folder to make it one. I want you to circle back to that and play with it in your mind. The abundance is visible all around us. Our friends, our family, our pets, our homes, our jobs, the list goes on and on. Money on the other hand...hmm...well, you might say it seems harder to grasp or come by.

However, when we allow our eyes to see it, Abundance is all around us. And, by the same token, we can see Money is all around us, too.

Whether you see .05 cents, 5.00 dollars, 50.00 dollars, 500.00 dollars, 5,000.00 dollars, 500,000.00 dollars, no matter where the zeroes land, it is all energy. When you align it up to the energy of Money, the zeroes are just that— energy. Easy enough to grasp.

But how many zeroes can you really let in?

Could you let in $5,000?

When I ask people, they usually answer right away with, "Sure I can." But the tricky part is when they place onto this belief their attachment of HOW to let it in.

One day I was thinking, sure, if $5,000 fell out of the sky, or if I found a bag of Money in my back yard with $5,000, it would be easy to accept. Next thing you know, I was sitting in my front of my new lawyer who had just told me she needed $5,500 to retain her. I wanted this lawyer, she was going to be my dragon lawyer. Except, I did not have $5,500 in my bank account.

Well, the Money was delivered lightning fast. Within minutes my very good friend had put $5,000 into my account. These were my contrast days, so naturally I was amazed I could manifest it so quickly. But, then it brought up the thought of *Could I accept this?* I didn't find it in my backyard, it didn't come out of the sky. Although, it did come out of the blue—Blue Money.

At first, it was difficult although there were no strings attached. I knew this. But it made me a little uneasy for me to accept Money from a friend. First, there is pride, second, you internally feel guilty. Then, as I sat with the thoughts and feelings of accepting the Money, I chose to open my eyes to *accept* that I could put all those feelings aside and *embrace* it all.

Not just the Money. But the energy.

The gift.

The receiving.

I told the Universe one day I would have the Money to pay her back and I intended it would not be a long time either. Sure enough, she was the first person I paid back...and I was able to gift her a bicycle on top of it.

When we receive with attachment, Money is sitting right there, saying, "Hey, you, here I am. I am ready to come in, but are you ready to let me in?"

When we show some love and appreciation to receiving Money, it responds, "Hey, you are loving your Money, let me show you other ways I can delight you. And here is more Money."

Every time Money showed up for me, I practiced and practiced the lessons that were being shown to me. It used to be challenging, but I persevered, and I now enjoy giving *and* receiving because I receive as much as I give. My following birthday was a trip to Switzerland with royal treatment. I could never have imagined in my wildest dreams I would be given such an amazing experience. But Money loves to delight!

There is another aspect of receiving which many people have a problem with, and it is allowing in the Money for your divine gifts. You can probably relate to those people who are sharing their divine gift to teach and feel guilty about charging for their services. I've been there, too.

This question is actually a very common thread throughout my coaching calls:

How do you feel about people who accept Money in exchange for spiritually based actions?

When I first started as a Reiki practitioner, not even a Reiki Master at the time, there were people who said things like, "You know, well, you have a gift to heal animals, could you do it for free?"

And it felt kind of odd to be asked that, but at the same time, it made me doubt whether I should be charging. We used to charge $35 a session. Thirty-five dollars, that was all. But, still, this question harped on me. It got me thinking one day. Okay, this is a spiritually based action I'm doing; however, I did go through training. I did pay for and took classes. On the other hand, I am on a spiritual journey. How much is all this worth?

I put it into another perspective by realizing that I'm a pharmacist, too. I get paid six figures, I went to school to get my doctorate degree, and I don't have any problem accepting a paycheck. What is the difference? None.

I read a book written by Doreen Virtue several years back which opened my eyes to realizing something very powerful and important pertaining to the exchange of spiritual service for Money. I learned that what we do from a spiritually based place, being present to serve, is worth something and is an energy exchange.

In the book, Doreen discussed that when we feel uncomfortable charging for our spiritual service, it was probably linked to a past life where we might have lived in a world where our food and our shelter was provided, so all we had to do was do what we love and that's it. Everything was provided for in exchange.

But, now we live in a time where we no longer live in a commune. We live in a society where we have utilities, we have a mortgage or rent, we need to buy groceries, we have credit card bills and loans, and we *need* to have a job which pays for it all.

What if instead of working at a job, or maybe even on the side of our regular job, we chose to be of service doing what we love, what our purpose is? It would still require an exchange of energy, or Money. There is nothing wrong in that.

And accepting Money or charging for services, should not be attached to guilt, to doubt, or anything negative. Both ends of the spectrum—the giver of spiritual services and the receiver of these services—should be in harmony with the exchange.

We are here to do what we love and to bring joy to others which in turn brings us joy. So, I think if you realize that when you love what you do then your primary focus is not Money-based. It is Love-based.

You will make the Money because this is the natural order of giving and receiving.

Allow me to presume that you are a natural giver and care greatly for others. This personality is in your soul, it is made up in your DNA, you want to help people. We don't want to block this, rather we want to maintain a balance which allows you to continue your service. Which is the receiving part. But so many people have uncomfortable feelings when they are receiving.

I want you to receive, and I want you to receive one hundred percent because your higher Self is already a spiritual teacher.

You are already a healer.

You are already a lightworker.

You are already a coach.

You have all these diving gifts already inside you.

And when receiving and giving are balanced, that is when you hear the divine messages—your intuition comes in. That is when you can be receptive. Otherwise, it is just like having a conversation where nobody is listening.

When you put a price on your services, you are giving value to your gift, and you are supported in so many important ways.

The Money you allow in allows you to devote more time to your healing and to your teaching practice. If you accept the exchange of

Money for your spiritual services, you could use the Money towards your students, your clients, and all the things you love that you are doing or want to do. Ultimately, when you have more Money, you could be donating to your charities or wherever you want to direct Money to.

On the other hand, if you don't accept the Money then you are going to have to spend more of your valuable time doing a job you possibly do not enjoy in order to earn it.

I like what Doreen wrote in her book, she says,

> *"Your past life time where you*
> *stood with a begging bowl is over.*
> *You are a professional who deserves*
> *remuneration for your work."*

Yes, you can be paid for your spiritual gifts.

You are following your divine purpose by tapping into your spiritual gifts.

We are all being of service to one another when we step into the realization of our own unique gifts and talents and exchange a balanced energy with one another, so we can continue to provide our unique gifts. Some gifts may appear to be the same, but our distinct qualities and attributes makes us all different. There is only one of you. There is only one of us each.

When you really start to look at yourself deep within and appreciate who you are, it will bring up all your gifts to the surface which will contribute towards your healing for receiving.

Earlier I disclosed that I had been given the experience of a trip to Switzerland for my birthday. Reflecting over that amazing trip, not only was it a birthday getaway, it was a time for being with friends and celebrating all life has to offer. There was such an outpouring of love in this circle of friendship.

My best friend was with me on this journey, and we met new friends who are now part of our family. It felt like we had been family for many lifetimes. It was pure joy, it was fun. We laughed so much. There was no stress, no strife, no struggling.

You might be wondering why I am sharing this with you here. It is important for me to share this because my entire journey, starting with Reiki Fur Babies, to being Present to Serve, to Money Alchemist, and everything in between, being involved in these spiritual services *is* what led me to Switzerland. I was given an opportunity to see how amazing the Universe is. My heart welled up with love and appreciation for everyone who made it all possible. And, also, with gratitude for myself and my gifts.

When we give, we can receive.

Yes, I love to give—it is one of my favorite acts of love to do, from a place of no hesitation. And receiving has become another one of my favorite things as well.

I have come to realize it really is a full circle—giving and receiving. It just keeps getting bigger and bigger, too. It is not just material things. Although, yes, they can be pretty awesome.

But giving and receiving is mainly about the bonding.

It is about the connection.

It is about the love.

We need more of this on our planet.

I hope you can feel the love I am sending you at this moment.

I am setting an intention that you, too, arrive full circle to your abundance.

Wherever you are reading this right now, I just ask you to take a deep breath and set an intention that you are open to stand into your authentic Self, fully, and recite:

I ask Spirit to let the divine gifts I was given shine and be seen. I ask Archangel Zadkiel to help me remember who I was before I came to this planet, what my soul journey is. I ask Archangel Zadkiel to bring me the support that I need whether it is in the form of Money, the right people, the perfect situation, and whatever is the perfect outcome for my highest good. I ask to have eyes to see the abundance that is around me continually. I ask that any fear which comes to me be transmuted to the highest vibration there is which is Love. I ask that I can love myself through all I have learned by being present to serve, and then as I enter the next transformative stage, to allow all my divine gifts to flow in. I ask and thank the Money Fairies for their special blessing upon me and upon all who have learned to be present to serve. And so it is.

Feel the presence of the energy from all sources vibrating and aligning you to the abundance which is already yours.

Close your eyes. Breathe. Feel.

Your Money blues are no more.

Everywhere you go, wherever you are, blue Money flows to you.

CH 9 ~ LAST BUT NOT LEAST,

HOW DO YOU KEEP THE MONEY

FLOWING IN?

I have spoken with many people from all walks of life, all different ages, college students, single mothers, single fathers, married couples and divorcees. Everyone wants to know how is it that I do what I do and, "How do we keep the Money flowing in...?"

My answer is the same every time, and still is. Anyone can do this. After all I did it. It wasn't too long ago when I wasn't sure how I was going to pay my mortgage, bills, buy food, some of the most basic things in life. And now, I'm living proof. This is what I tell my clients:

- **Find out what lights you up**. What is it that gives you joy? Hikes in nature, running, cooking, random acts of kindness, dog walks, volunteer work, teaching, hanging out with friends, music, reading, etc. Whatever it is, do more of it. For me, it is connection—I love talking to people about anything spiritual, creating what we want in our lives, spending time with my pets, yoga, meditation. Go on a discovery to find your most joyful activity and do more of what ignites that glowing spark in you.

- **Flowing appreciation to where you are and what you are doing**. Another big key is whatever it is that you are doing, flow BIG Love to it, see the good in whatever your situation is. Flowing more and more appreciation. If you're going through a hard time, allow those feelings to come up, feel them and then release them. It is okay. Everything doesn't have to feel "perfect" all the time. Flowing some love to your bills, when your bills come, feels better to say, "Yay, I have Money to pay my bills." When I get a bill from my VA, I pay it within seconds. Because I appreciate my VA and I appreciate the Money that comes in to pay her. Change the feeling of fear and lack to appreciation and love. Another thing I did when I first moved to a new state, I chose to see all the good in it. When it was raining constantly, I chose to see how green and lush it is up here.

- **Support. Know you ARE supported. Call in your divine team**. We talked about the angels, fairies, elementals. They are all a good thing. Or, call your coach. We are never alone. Support is very important, to have someone on your side, cheering you on. Especially when manifesting Money.

- **Tapping into the NOW. Truly living in the MOMENT**. One of the most effective ways I tapped into abundance, and Money kept coming in, was I never looked beyond today, only at what was evidently in front of me. I did not know how I was going to pay my mortgage, but I just lived in the moment. My brother said to me one day, "Don't you think you should be more practical and have a plan?" I told him, "If I look beyond today, I'll never be able to sleep."

- **Not being attached to the HOW it is coming**. But trusting that it is. When you have no attachment, is when the miracles come in. I never dreamed this is how it would be that Money came in for me. I am still amazed when I receive Blue Money. I continue to live like this and amazing things keep coming in.

- **Checking into your vibration. Keeping it loose and light, having fun**. If you're feeling good play the Money game, just remember it is a game. If it feels good, do a vision board. You can create secret boards on Pinterest or make one and pin it up on your wall at home. You can write intentions in your journal. Write love notes to Money. Lately, I have been singing to Money.

- **Being conscious. Paying attention to what is around you**. This is a more recent focus for me because I was trying to see what exactly it is I've been doing to bring in the abundance or feeling abundant, and then realized that when I brought my awareness to my surroundings and to what was happening when Money came, it made me more present to receive MORE Money.

- **SELF LOVE IS THE KEY!** Last, but certainly not least. Make time for yourself, find that sacred place. Meditation. Self-love is the key to abundance. Nurturing yourself. You can manifest anything if you practice self-love. Being loving to yourself is the sure way to have Money come in faster.

CONCLUSION

My intention for writing *Money Blues to Blue Money* was to help you align yourself to Money thereby creating an everlasting flow of Money, so this is ideal to share with you.

I was going through some papers one night when I came across an old email printout I had sent to my ex-husband a long time ago. It totally cracked me up! It was an email on how to be a Powerful Money Magnet. Ha!

I was taken aback, because even during that time, when I still wasn't doing Money alchemy, something was already brewing inside me. But, I didn't recall the email at all. What matters now is that this message is for everyone. Here's what it said:

1. Be clear about the amount of Money you want to receive. State it and intend it. (Not how much you earn, but how much you want to receive)

2. Fall in love with Money. (Most people don't love Money because they think they won't ever have enough of it.)

3. Visualize and imagine yourself spending all the Money you want as though you have it already.

4. Speak, act, and think from the mindset of being wealthy now.

5. Do not speak or think of the lack of Money for a single second.

6. Be grateful for the Money you have. Appreciate it as you touch it.

7. Make lists of all the things you will buy with an abundance of Money.

8. Do whatever it takes for you to feel wealthy.

9. Affirm to yourself every day that you have an abundance of Money and that it comes to you effortlessly.

10. Appreciate all the riches around you, including the riches of others. Look for wealth wherever you go and appreciate it.

11. Ask yourself often during the day, *Am I attracting more Money now or pushing it away with my thoughts?* It will help you become aware when you fall off track, so you can realign quickly.

12. Be certain Money is coming to you.

13. Love yourself and know you are deserving and worthy of an abundance of Money.

14. Always pay yourself first from your wage then your creditors.

15. Remind yourself every day you are a Money magnet. Repeat, I am a Money magnet and Money comes to me effortlessly and easily.

16. Write out a check to yourself for the sum of Money you would like to have and carry it in your wallet. Look at it often.

17. Do whatever it takes to feel good. Emotions of joy and happiness are powerful.

18. Love yourself!

Play with these Money magnet tips and pick the ones you feel you resonate with. Or use them all. More importantly, Have FUN!

Money loves to play and have fun.

And it loves surprising you out of the blue...

That's Blue Money.

Thoughts & Notes:

More from Dr. Ming Chee can be found on The Money Alchemist website: www.themoneyalchemist.com. You may follow her on social media via Facebook (Ming Chee) and Instagram (ReikiFurBabies). She may also be contacted through email at: ming@themoneyalchemist.com.

63528739R00085

Made in the USA
Middletown, DE
06 February 2018